The *Mystery* and *Miracle* of New Birth

How Children of Men Become Sons and Daughters of God

UCHE C. EKEH

First Edition 2014
ISBN-13:   978-3-347-35989-5   [Paperback Edition]
                 978-3-347-35993-2   [eBook Edition]

Library of Congress Control Number: 2014949525

Dedication

This book is dedicated to my mother's last born brother, Mr. Joseph Anukwu, fondly known as Uncle Joe. Uncle Joe is a humble, Christian, husband—and—father, a man of unquestionable character toward God and his family. His simple faith and loyalty to Jesus Christ continues to amaze his friends and the rest of us who are acquainted with him. Much love to you Uncle Joe.

Introduction

*T*he *Mystery and Miracle of New Birth*: *How Children of Men Become Sons and Daughters of God* was written to be provocative to believers. It challenges Christians to bring the letters of the Scripture in conformity with the Spirit of the Scripture. To an outside observer of Christianity, it may appear as if the Scriptures promise much more than it can deliver. Others might use religious platitudes to explain away the concern as irrelevant because God is holy and man is vile. Also, some might feel offended that the Scripture is being insulted by this kind of suggestion. Believe it or not, this is not the first time someone wondered why stories of past victories do not match current needs among the people of God. In the Old Testament, Gideon was a man acquainted with great stories of how God delivered Israel from Egyptian slavery and bondage, and how He later drove the Canaanite nations out of their land and gave their land to Israel. He remembered the story so vividly that when the Medianites began to exert similar dominance over Israel, Gideon wondered out loud if indeed the stories he had been told were authentic and believable. As a result of his speculation and quandary, the Spirit of God thrust him in the forefront as a warrior leader and God used him to accomplish a great feat in the nation during his generation. Gideon, the man who, ironically, disqualified himself and his clan from leadership authority and responsibility, becomes God's anointed deliverer who rescued Israel from her arch enemies. Now, if there is a Gideon inside or outside the church, this is your season to shine because the church needs you.

Generally speaking, John 3:16 is an evangelistic vignette, popularized by America's venerable Pastor Rev. Billy Graham, but there is more to that Scripture than evangelism. Not to diminish the significance of evangelism, it needs to be said that there is nothing in the gospel closer to the heart of God than to bring souls into His Kingdom. Therefore, John 3:16 remains a call, and the echo of an invitation from God to mankind to become His sons and daughters after the "order of Jesus". And God did not anticipate religion when He issued the call but He knew Satan will not rest until he finds a way to corrupt what is holy and righteous. Religion is a corruption of what is holy and true. Religion is man's invention to evade obedience to the Word of God while pretending to be in relationship with God. Christianity beckons the world to God, then and now, and there is no substitute for a relationship with God outside the walls of Christianity.

Salvation is wholly and essentially supernatural. The birth of Jesus at the manger in Bethlehem, Israel, was and still is, a supernatural event no less in significance than the new birth of a child of God into His Kingdom through repentance. This book aims to challenge Christians—those truly born-again and spirit-filled—to see both events as one and the same. Jesus came from heaven to earth to dwell with man and the Christian went from earth into heaven to dwell with God & among the heavenly hosts. It is just a matter of order, by the God of order. Jesus said that one must be born again to see and must be born of water and Spirit to enter. While seeing precedes entering, there can be no entering without seeing. In other words, one can see, yet, not able to enter. If so, there might be men and women walking around the Kingdom of God who are not in the Kingdom. Well, this book exposes the fallacy and seeks to correct it by redirecting attention to the original command given by the Lord Himself.

Now, about sons and daughters of God, this book clearly shows that all children of Abraham are children of God, but not all Abraham's children are sons and daughters of God. There is a difference, and the distinction matters. This book points to Jesus as the sum and substance of what it means to be a son or daughter of God. A son of God has no prized instrument in his possession to enter into negotiations with God. It is obedience to the Word of God all the way! God's will prevails in all matters of importance to His Kingdom, and such is the oath of sons and daughters of God. Just as Jesus is made a priest forever after the order of

Melchizedek, so are the sons and daughters of God after the order of Jesus. When one becomes a son of God, there is no looking back. Scripture says: "No one, having put his hand to the plow, and looking back, is fit for the Kingdom of God" (Lk.9:62). This book reminds readers that authority and responsibility are inherent with the title of *sons and daughters of God*. This book is a call to action. Gideon wondered about God and He made him a warrior and a winner. Jesus Christ can do the same with the church— the called out ones who also are the called – just as He did in former days.

Chapter One

In The Mind of God is The Mystery of New Birth

The coming of Jesus into the world was, and still is, a phenomenal event unlike any other event that has ever occurred on the earth since its creation. For the first time in the history of creation, the Almighty God took residence among His people, most specifically through His only begotten Son, Jesus, to dwell with His people on the earth. Through this act of grace, He gave further insight and illustration of His love for mankind, and thus, revealed His desire to bring humanity into an eternal love relationship with Himself. In God's mind, He needs sons and daughters to populate paradise and the process of redemption and salvation is how He does it. Consider for a moment what the book of Job says about the mind of God: "Can you search out the deep things of God? Can you find out the limits of the Almighty? They are higher than heaven – what can you do? Deeper than Sheol – what can you know? Their measure is longer than the earth and broader than the sea" (Job 11:7-9). The mind of God is the inexhaustible wonder of knowledge and wisdom which man cannot comprehend. Without any argument, it is precisely so.

Consequently, the advent of Jesus into the earthly realm still remains an open invitation of love from the Almighty God to mankind, to join the heavenly- spiritual family of God in anticipation of the imminent return of His Son. This is the mystery of the love of God which He proclaimed over humanity that whosoever believes in Him should not perish but have everlasting life. God is Love. He is the author and giver of life. Is it just everlasting life or is there something more to it? Undoubtedly, God is usually up to something all the time. Besides an everlasting relationship with God, He also proposes to resolve, through the gospel of His Son, the universal man's perennial obsession with immortality once and for all. Generations before the birth of Jesus Christ, and after, have searched for ways to become one with the Almighty God through human sacrifices and blood covenants. Evidently, it did not work then and doesn't work now because God was not about to permit Satan to realize, through trickery and more deception, the goal of his failed coup. Furthermore, every event in the history of creation is already preset by Him and each event must follow His schedule. Before the time of the Son of God, access into eternity and the presence of God was quite limited to certain individuals, but when the Son of God came, the way to immortality became an essential tenet in the mystery and miracle of new birth granted to those who believe. In 2Timothy 1:8-10, the apostle Paul writes: "Therefore do not be ashamed of the testimony of our Lord, nor of me His prisoner, but share with me in the sufferings for the gospel according to the power of God, who has saved us and called us with a holy calling, not according to our works, but according to His own purpose and grace which was given to us in Christ Jesus before time began, but has now been revealed by the appearing of our Savior Jesus Christ, who has abolished death and brought immortality to light through the gospel". Man was not made to die. It was sin that brought corruption and death to humanity. Finally, Jesus restored life and immortality to mankind through His gospel.

Long before the birth of Jesus, the universal man had nurtured a deep preoccupation with immortality apart from the wisdom and will of God. This preoccupation with immortality leading to divinity for mankind quite possibly originated with Satan during his failed coup attempt when he sought to become like the Most High. Evidently, it conforms to his second lie to Eve in the Garden of Eden as recorded in the book of Genesis: "For God knows that in the day you eat of it your eyes will be opened, and you will be like God, knowing good and evil" (Gen.3:5). Although he was cast out of heaven and into the open air to become a disembodied spirit, he continues to step up attacks against anything that is God's—especially mankind who represents God choicest creation.

Though the Son of God describes him as "a liar and the father of it" (Jn.8:44), his derangement, nevertheless, is diagnosable. First, when he rebelled against God and was cast out of heaven, God exorcised him from the assembly of loyal worshippers and permanently replaced him with believers. Secondly, when he deceived Eve in the Garden of Eden, an event which precipitated the fall, God stripped him of power and authority over the universe and permanently invested the same in man. As we move on, you will discover how the unfolding of events made Satan miserably mad against man, and his determination to distract, harass and corrupt his mind toward God. In the meantime, the Son of God—Jesus—God in the flesh, who was manifested to rectify and put an end to all the lies of Satan once and for all, diligently obeyed the commands of the Father and fulfilled every letter of ordinance and word of God to appease the heart of the Father. Humanity would not need to fantasize about immortality and divinity any longer because such privileges are vested in the mystery and the miracle of new birth, through the gospel of the Son of God. John, the revelator, was in agreement on this matter when he wrote: "He who sins is of the devil, for the devil has sinned from the beginning. For this purpose the Son of God was manifested that He might destroy the works of the devil" (1 Jn.3:8). Herein rests the mystery and the miracle of new birth.

Adam was the first man, created in the image and likeness of God, but Adam was disobedient to the instructions of God. Of course, the failure of Adam is not to be attributed to God because "All the works of His hands are verity and justice. All His precepts are sure. They stand fast forever and ever, and are done in truth and uprightness" (Ps.111: 7-8). Adam failed in carrying out the specific instructions of God not to eat of the tree of the knowledge of good and evil because he unfortunately exercised his choice to disobey the word of God. Adam's fault in the fall was both direct and indirect. Up until that moment in the history of creation, Adam was familiar with the voice of God and his own voice. He certainly ought to have recognized the strangeness of the counter voice and questioned its authenticity but he went along with it as though it did not matter. Well, look at where we were after the fall and thereafter.

Moreover, when God gave instructions to Adam, his wife Eve, had not yet been created. The instruction to not eat from the tree of knowledge of good and evil was from God to Adam, and that alone should have caused him to question the source of the information countering God's command. If only he had sought verification of that information from his beloved wife, perhaps, there might not have been the fall as we know it. Furthermore, Adam's absence during Eve's encounter with Satan was troubling. Had Adam been present during the encounter, he could have objected to Satan's suggestion because God had directly and plainly instructed him not to eat from the tree of the knowledge of good and evil. Besides, there were plentiful fruits, edible fruits in the Garden of Eden that the eventual fall was not a matter of appetite or hunger but of naivety and lust. They did not have the need to desire the fruit of the tree of knowledge of good and evil if Satan, in his obsession and complex to instigate prematurity in God's creative order, had not misled them.

But Jesus, who is the second and last Adam, came and declared, "Then I said, Behold, I have come – in the volume of the book it is written of Me – to do Your will, oh God." (Heb.10:7). He did not come to fulfill part of the ordinances or sections of the Law of God, but the whole book of the law. It was that kind of loyalty to the word and instruction of God that burned in the heart of Jesus, which caused Him to say at His temptation by Satan that "Man shall not live by bread alone, but by every word that proceeds from the mouth of God" (Matt. 4:4). To be a reflection of God is the radical nature of a Son of God, and the life of Jesus typifies that kind of radical commitment to His Father. The same point is illustrated in another place in the Scriptures, when Jesus equates doing the will of God as food for Him. "My food is to do the will of Him who sent Me, and to finish His work" (Jn.4:34). Such a commitment is also expected of sons and daughters of God after Him. Jesus carried out His role and responsibility to God and to man, to the extent that everything that needs to be done by Him was done. In the end, He could declare, "It is finished" (Jn.19:30). What was finished? The work of redemption and salvation was finished. Therefore, humanity's quest to be one with God was completely and finally resolved by the coming of Jesus into the world. It was settled for all eternity that man, like God, would live forever. The universal man no longer has need for satanic rituals, or blood covenants with other humans or animals to achieve eternal life. For, there is no life in any other name other than in Jesus. The "promise of life" is in Jesus Christ alone (2 Tim.1:1). Religion is lifeless. The invitation to join the family of God has been given to human beings all over the world, and that invitation stands until Jesus returns to earth and establish His rule and dominion.

Salvation was first a mystery in the mind of God before it became a miracle because it was Almighty God who manifested Himself in Jesus for the purpose of redemption and reconciliation with sinful humanity. Come to think of it, did God have to become Man made for the cross to reconcile humanity with Himself? Apparently so, otherwise how else could God find a fitting sacrifice that would appease His heart and permanently cover all the sins of humanity's past, present and future? Besides, how else could one understand and appreciate the mystery and the miracle of new birth where God became Man for God so that Man can be God to man if redemption and salvation were not settled once and for all? For the purpose of redemption and salvation "God became Man to God so that Man can be God to man." Jesus the Christ of God became a Man for the cross and after His death, burial, resurrection, and ascension into heaven He became the absolute Lord and Savior in heaven, on the earth and beneath the earth.

The Christian concept of the new-birth, or born-again experience, did not begin with the conversation between Jesus and Nicodemus in the New Testament. It was all in the mind of God long before the Nicodemus exchange. The mind of God as previously mentioned is a sea of knowledge and information. If we had all the time in the world to explore His mind, we would go on for all of eternity before ever getting to the point of describing what the mind of God is capable of. Even after giving due diligence to all the available revelations of God (from every created thing in the past and to the present moment), He still remains the biggest and most complicated mystery in the world which He created. God's mind is unfathomable. It was God's idea to raise up sons and daughters after His only begotten Son— Jesus—which provides humanity with the miracle of new birth. Jesus is the prototypical specimen of the new breed of believers in God, those who would eventually become sons and daughters of God to finish the work which Jesus started. The Son of God is unlike the off-spring of Adam and Eve, who are mired in rebellion against the word of God, but in every way similar to the sons and daughters of God who are being called out to lead the rest of the unsaved worldwide to embrace the teachings of Jesus Christ in the gospel.

It must be clear that God wasn't surprised that Adam would not put up a fight or any resistance to keep the serpent out of the Garden of Eden and away from Eve. Adam was complicit in the sin of Eve. And, the subsequent pronouncement by God (to the first family and to Satan) of what He had determined to do in order to do away with satanic opposition to the will of the Father was made public that moment. Here is the pronouncement against Satan: "Because you have done this, you are cursed more than all cattle, and more than every beast of the field; on your belly you shall go, and you shall eat dust all the days of your life. And I will put enmity between you and the woman, and between your seed and her seed. He shall bruise your head and you shall bruise his heal" (Gen. 3:14-15). Thus, began the declaration and the preparation of the battle of the ages, which was scheduled be to be fought somewhere down the ages in God's scheme of events. Meanwhile, God continued His work, by stealth you might say. He weaved and crafted His way in a series of events, from Noah through Abraham and finally, the Man—Jesus, in the New Covenant era. This epic "battle of the ages" ensued with the coming of Jesus, born to the family of Joseph and Mary in the city of Bethlehem, the city of David. The Son of God—the Christ of God—came down to earth, and took upon Himself the nature of Man, guaranteeing absolute victory over the forces of darkness and, thus, returned dominion of the earth to man, just as the Father intended from the very beginning.

And what better way to execute the war of the ages than to bring man (the very object of the battle) into it and make him ruler over Satan (and all his forces of darkness)? Satan was the one who initially sought to subjugate and humiliate man in the things of life and in the Kingdom of God. The fact that Satan's head was bruised in the battle confirms why he is such a nuisance who would not quit deceiving and himself being deceived even by the ones he seeks to control. Although the battle is spiritual, it is no less warfare than conventional warfare. The exception is that "the weapons of our warfare are not carnal but mighty in God for pulling down strong-holds" (2 Cor. 10:4) or satanic schemes and devices that keep people oppressed and depressed. It is immaterial to Satan whom he uses or what he uses as long as he can keep any individual from knowing and fulfilling the will of God. That is his top priority. God's goal in the battle is to eradicate evil in the world, not by His act alone but through the resistance of men and women who reject Satan's ways.

Though the deceiver may be unrelenting is his mission to deceive mankind with any tool available to him, the church of Jesus Christ has the Scriptures—the eternal Word of God—and the Spirit of God to guide her to develop sound doctrines. The Word of God is the surest tool – basic instruction before leaving earth (bible) – a proven material to minister to the needs of people in the church and outside the church for righteous and victorious Christian living. Without the counsel of God in His word, how can the church be relevant in a society that is obsessed with redefining what is right and true? Besides the Scriptures, the Holy Spirit is also given with the same purpose: to guide and direct the church in the business of the Kingdom of God— the saving of souls. Consequently, the church must refrain from unbiblical doctrine whose credence and verity hang on denominational platitudes, rather than the revealed word of God. The church should thoroughly teach and explain the Scriptures in light of the apostle Paul's admonition to his spiritual son, Timothy, in 2 Timothy 3:16-17. It serves no useful purpose for either the churched or the un-churched that Christians read from the same passages in Scripture and come away with divergent conclusions or interpretations. It ought not to be so, but it is because the Holy Spirit is scarcely at work in the hearts and minds of some in the church. Those in the church who seem quite content with denominational traditions and pageantry seem less perturbed by the flood of political correctness, or rather, religious correctness, destroying the spiritual vitality of the church. Human knowledge and understanding of Scripture is woefully inadequate, and essentially misleading, without the guidance of the Holy Spirit. He is the author of the Bible, and who can explain the

Scriptures better to the human mind than He? He is the author and creator of all things, including man. This is why doctrine matters! It matters to God and it should matter to the church. Proper doctrine will produce sound and effective witness for the Kingdom of God.

In Luke 24:49, the Bible says: "Behold, I send the promise of my Father upon you; but tarry in the city of Jerusalem until you are endued with power from on high". Now consider the definition of the gospel by the apostle Paul in the first chapter of his epistle to the Romans: "For I am not ashamed of the gospel of Christ, for it is the power of God to salvation for everyone who believes, for the Jew first and also for the Greek [Gentile]" (Rom.1:16). Both the gift of the Holy Spirit and the gospel of Jesus the Christ, represent gifts of power to the church, and we cannot have one without the other. The power, and the demonstration of it, must be emphasized in the preaching of the gospel because the anointing rests on the word of God. In Acts1:4, Jesus strongly appealed to the apostles not to leave the city of Jerusalem until the gift of God, which is the gift of power, manifest Himself upon them. They believed him, and the result was Pentecost. Without the Pentecostal experience, and all the charismatic gifts of the spirit (1 Cor. 12:8 -10), it is altogether impossible to serve God in the demonstration of His power. Those who leave the "city of Jerusalem" without the outpouring of the gift of God from on high will do the work of the ministry in the strength and power of their own minds, and the apostles knew that and so remained in Jerusalem until the outpouring. If the Holy Spirit was indispensable to the Son of God, and subsequently, to His apostles to fulfill their assignments, the same is equally true for *all* contemporary believers. And even more so now, due to our sinful environment and borderless digital global villages and towns of the present time. It is a place where criminal activity is coordinated by criminal elements from one part of the globe to the other. That is why God became Man in the form of Jesus, the Son, in obedience to God, the Father, so that Jesus would become God to man (humanity). Jesus came and took all of our sins upon Himself, and offered His sinless nature and divinity to us, thus equipping us to do our part in the kingdom of God as we await His return.

Chapter Two

The God of Order

The world as we know it is an ordered universe. It is a world of order, with inviolable principles, whether in obscurity or in plain view, and anyone who violates its laws shall not escape the consequences for his or her rebellion, by the order of God. He, Himself, is the God of order. And, the world's wisest man, Solomon, concurred: "He who digs a pit will fall into it. And whoever breaks through a wall will be bitten by a serpent" (Eccl.10:8). The weight of the universe rests on the word of God –Living and Written. Those who scoff at the Bible as a book of antiquity will discover no manual or publication that rivals the Bible in its capacity to offer hope and assurance in a world full of chaos and agony. The Bible still is God's official autography for all Christians (e.g. Roman Catholics, Eastern Orthodox, Protestant believers, etc.), and one wonders how the church could read the same book and still come away with meanings that cannot be substantiated from that very same book.

Years ago, the Holy Spirit spoke clearly into my spirit, at a time when I was pondering how the Almighty God in all of His powerful attributes could become God in the flesh, and dwell with man for the redemption and salvation of man. Without much struggle, the response of the Holy Sprit came roaring back to me. The Spirit of God said, "God became Man to God so that Man can be God to man". Meaning: God became Man, in the person of Jesus the Son, in obedience to God the Father, so that Jesus would become savior to mankind. Now, consider this: God is Almighty and eternal; He is Omnipotent, Omnipresent and Omniscient. The path to granting divinity to man was crystal clear to Him before creation. The path toward redemption and salvation were established by Him. And because the goal was to grant dominion of the earth back to man, the plan could not, and would not fail. Therefore, Christ—the eternal Son of God, assumed the role of man in order to enter the realm of the physical world as Jesus, completely God and completely Man (Col. 2:9) to conduct this "special operations" and to finish it forever in heaven, on earth, and even below the earth. Jesus, today, is Lord of all and the Savior of mankind. He is now God to man because only He could appease the heart of God, fulfill every ordinance of the Old Covenant (the entire Law of Moses and the prophets) through His death, burial, resurrection and ascension into heaven. And now a Man sits, eternally, at the right hand of God—the Man—Jesus!

After the Holy Spirit spoke into my heart, believe me, I felt as though my international ministry was about to be launched within the next hour or on the following day, but as you can see, hope springs eternal! Each time I attempted to share this revelation with other Christians, the most I would get is a nod, and my heart would sink because something that caused my heart to throb with joy and excitement was a non-sequitur to others. The whole idea of a Holy God mingling with sinful humanity is completely at odds with our human minds and religious sophistication. The only way to make sense of it is to imagine what the love of God for man was worth to Him— the death of His Son on the cross, which now gives us an evaluation of the soul being saved.

As you ponder this idea and become awe-struck, you may scream, "blasphemy" at the author but be aware that it is God who longs for man, who seeks to make Himself known to man, and not the other way around, as some of us would like to believe. God is always seeking to reveal Himself to the choicest of His creation—man—but, unfortunately, man appears to be busy for other things more than God, the only One who is actually able to satisfy all the cravings of the heart. Long before it enters the heart of man to seek God, God has been working His way from the invisible realm into the visible realm, to reveal Himself to man as a benevolent God because He is good and forever so. As Scripture confirms, "For the Son of Man has come to seek and to save the lost" (Lk.19:10). "But God demonstrates His own love toward us, in that while we were still sinners, Christ died for us" (Rom.5:8).

You see, it is not man finding God, as we quite often and religiously claim: "When I found the Lord…" It is never man finding God, but God who, in His mercy and love for humanity, seeks man out. The decision was made before there was a concept of time, and so was our salvation accomplished in Christ before there was time (Eph. 1:4; 2 Tim.1:9; Rom.16:23 and Jer. 1:5). After all, it is the Holy Spirit, the author of the Bible, who said that Jesus came to seek and to save the lost, and we must believe Him.

Humanity worldwide is lost without Jesus Christ. That is not good news for anyone whose heart and mind is torn and twisted by the effects of sin. This has nothing to do with religion if one considers religion as a sacred obligation, or how religious one might be, or could become. There is a measure of blindness among people who reject the message of the gospel because the gospel of the Son of God runs counter to the natural instincts of man. The gospel is spiritual and cannot be understood by a carnal mind without the Holy Spirit (1 Cor. 2:14). Simply put, religion is man's way of seeking to please God, while Christianity is God's way of establishing a relationship of love with man. This can only happen through Jesus Christ, and by the power of the Holy Spirit. This is what separates Christianity from religion and makes it distinctly supernatural. Christianity is not a religion, but a relationship proffered by God to humanity, through Jesus Christ, and by the power of the Holy Spirit. God the Father, God the Son, and God the Holy Spirit are equal and the same, and where One is, the others are equally present. These three represent the council of heaven. Salvation is a gift and also a miracle. Without the shed blood of Jesus, and His death on the cross of Calvary, there is no redemption.

The mystery of the "new" man is to make man unconquerable, just like the Son of God Himself was during His earthly ministry. If the church gets this message, then the church will experience a surge of power and fresh revelation for its purpose, duties and responsibilities to God and to humanity. The church will rediscover its very foundation: "upon this rock I will build My church and the gates of hell shall not prevail against it" (Matt.16:18). Now, think of the church as those who are called out individually or on a larger scale, a community of people called out by God, to labor and to facilitate the process of bringing others into the Kingdom of God. Christian evangelism is based on sharing one's experience of deliverance from sin, so that others experiencing similar challenges could receive the same miracle of deliverance, which the Lord has already afforded to believers.

The life that one lives after salvation matters. Someone, somewhere, is watching to see evidence of a new lifestyle, a direct result of the application of the word of God and its power to resolve the delicate issues of life. The affected ones will use it as their motivation to make the same commitment to Jesus for a new life. The word of God, and the indwelling Spirit of God, both provide spiritual insight and wisdom for daily living. Again, here is one more reason God (Christ) became Man for God (the Father), so that Man (Jesus) can become God to man (humanity). He gives to man, through the Holy Spirit, the strength and wisdom to live in the here-and-now. In God's thinking, there is not a "cartoonish character" believer who was not predestined to be conformed to the image of His Son. That is why Jesus died a brutal and ignoble death on the cross. Thereby, creating a new race of people, equipped with every spiritual gift to defeat and demolish satanic strongholds during the course of life and ministry for the Kingdom of God. It cost God His own life on the cross of Cavalry to redeem and to save man from his sin. We do not have to quarrel or stumble over the idea of God dying on the cross because, as Jesus said: "I have power to lay it down [His life], and I have power to take it [up] again. This command I have received from My Father" (Jn.10:18). So whether there are some in the church living beneath their privileged position, or above it, the issue of where one is resides with man. The death, burial and resurrection of Jesus from the dead in some ways still remain a mystery, but certainly a mystery unveiled.

According to the apostle Peter, "His divine power has given to us all things that pertain to life and godliness, through the knowledge of Him who called us by glory and virtue: by which have been given to us exceeding great and precious promises, that through these you may be partakers of the divine nature, having escaped the corruption that is in the world through lust" (2 Pet.1:3-4). Therefore, the mystery surrounding the new birth experience can be unearthed in the decision of the council of heaven to send the Word of God down to the realm of the earth (a realm of sin, debauchery, and all kinds of limitations), in the fullness of time, to reveal the Father and open the door for a loving, covenant relationship with the Almighty and His children. In this covenantal relationship, the stronger pledges to do for the weaker, what the weaker is unable to do for itself. Now that is something to cheer about!

God is the author of eternal, covenantal relationship between man and Himself, a covenant He sealed with the blood of His only begotten Son. The Son of God had to conquer all the oppositional forces of Satan, and his influence on mankind (the flesh), before He could settle down to rule. He had to overcome principalities and powers before He was granted all authority to rule, in heaven and on earth, and also beneath the earth. And the same vision remains and awaits every believer who steps into the same ministry with Him. This makes Christianity a bold and conquering force over demonic forces. The victories of the Messiah are the victories of the sons and daughters of God, who through the indwelling Spirit of Christ, embrace the call of God. Today, a Man is seated at the right hand of God in Heaven, the Man—Jesus, who is now God to mankind. Even while the Christian, or at least some Christians, are still feeling their way through the domains of earthly life, He has uplifted us and made us kings, priests, heirs, and joint heirs of all that is God's, and made us sit together with Christ in the heavenly place (Rom.8:17; Eph.2:6).

Now consider this: the Father would give nothing to the Son that He would withhold from the rest of the sons and daughters of His Kingdom. If Jesus— the Christ—is the fullness of the Godhead, and He is the head of all principality and power, might and dominion, visible and invisible, in the heavens and on the earth, even beneath the earth, and the believer is complete in Him, what then has God left to chance? What is the Christian not able to overcome in life through the power of the indwelling Spirit of Christ when the Christian seeks and enters the rest which He gives? Yes, there is a rest which God gives, and that is the ultimate place of victory in Him. Doesn't this explain why God is the Alpha, the Omega, the First and the Last, the Beginning and the End, and absolutely nothing is left to chance? This is what Satan is incensed about with God. God covers us with His Presence and satan can not attack and destroy at his own whim. The master of illusion and prematurity always seeks to disrupt deliberate eternal timetable and impose corruption in God's eternal perfect schedule of events, and cause people not to reach and fulfill life's purposes. This further illustrates the point that God became Man (Jesus) for God, so that Man (Jesus) can be God to man (humanity). The heavy lifting was completed by the Son of God and our job is to do a "mop-up operation" and "keep the house clean" for His eventual return.

Redemption cost God everything He had, so that man could become co-regent with God, both in heaven and on the earth. Do not forget that believers are destined to judge those who would reject God's proffered gift to humanity, including the angels in the millennial reign of Christ (1 Cor. 6:3-4). The prophet Obadiah saw this new thing, this new phenomena, which God had determined to do during the time of his writing when he said, "Then many saviors shall come to Mount Zion to judge the mountains of Esau, and the Kingdoms shall be the Lord's" (Obad.1:21). Mount Zion is the prophetic term for the church of the Firstborn, the born-again and spirit-filled sons and daughters of God, after the order of Jesus.

Back again to the nightly encounter between Jesus and Nicodemus, as recorded in the gospel of John, the Jewish leader, Nicodemus, approached Jesus and offered a tepid endorsement of the unusual nature of His ministry. The Jewish leader also acknowledged the diverse kinds of miracles people witness in Jesus' ministry. In reply, Jesus said to him, "Most assuredly I say to you, unless one is born again, he cannot **see** the Kingdom of God" (Jn.3:3). Here, the Son of God unequivocally reminded the Jewish leader of the requirement for anyone to be considered a child of God. As you can see from Jesus' answer, there is an anticipation that those who seek to enter the Kingdom of God, must first, be born again. This was a "new" term for a new thing in the Kingdom of God as at the time. An un-regenerated mind is completely blind in spiritual matters, until the Son of God takes residence in the sinner and begins to open his spiritual understanding to the existence of spiritual matters. Education has great value in its prior and contemporary applications, and is necessary for human enlightenment in all intellectual matters, but only biblical education, with spiritual revelation, can equip followers of Jesus Christ for the Kingdom of God and for the benefit of humanity. Education by itself is useful and can be very valuable in dealing with natural challenges, but it is not the answer in the area of Godly wisdom. And ignorance is not any better.

Early in the book of Genesis we noticed a plurality in the personalities involved in creation. If the personality of the Godhead was of a singular being, it would be utterly useless to address the Godhead as "Us" instead of "Me" or "I." The point is that the second person in the Godhead existed with the Father and the Holy Spirit before creation. His name then was, and still is, the Word of God, Messiah, or the Christ. At that time, the name "Jesus" never existed as a personality except in the mind of the Father, Christ, and the Holy Spirit. The name of the man, Jesus, is subsumed in His mission as the Savior of man. The principle that the Son of God who was, and is, can now be applied to humanity in the same sense that man who was born of woman can now be born of God. Christ is not the last name of Jesus, but rather a combination of His title as Savior and Redeemer of His people. Knowing what happened to Jesus is relevant and indispensable for all who dare to follow in the steps of the Master.

There was an exchange, of some sort, in almost all the events in the life of Jesus, and this also is true with the rest of the sons and daughters of God. The Christ of God left His place in Glory, came down to the earth to become the Son of Man, and as a consequence, opened the door for believers to become sons and daughters of God. Consequently, believers now have their citizenship in heaven, more so than on earth. He became the Son of Man, so that those who believe in Him would become sons of God. He died on the cross of Cavalry for our sins, so that believers might live in true holiness and righteousness for God. He became poor, so that believers might become rich through His poverty. "Because as He is, so are we in this world" (1 Jn. 4:17). These are some of the great exchanges between Jesus and mankind. He allows mankind to become winners and overcomers in this life and in the life to come because He first overcame. One cannot be averse to prosperity, even if prosperity is limited to money alone, and pretend to be a servant of God in the Kingdom of God if it takes money to minister and to serve others. It is not enough to simply offer lip-service to the dire needs of humanity (both their physical and spiritual needs) when one cannot provide some of the basic needs to those in need. Besides, money is a good thing, not an evil thing. Jesus never said that money is evil. Only the love of money is condemned in Scripture. Service is about giving, and one cannot give something one does not have. God could not own the whole universe and deny His heirs pieces of His creations for a better life. Redemption is incomplete without deliverance from lack and poverty, which is what compelled Jesus to preach the gospel to the poor. This should also compel Christians to preach the gospel to the poor, and rescue them from their destruction. Proverbs 10:15 says, "The destruction of the poor is their poverty."

Chapter Three

Why Born Again?

So far, we have endeavored to make the case for the Christian doctrine of new birth, and in so doing advance the notion that there is no other biblical teaching for coming into a relationship with God other than the command to be born again. Church tradition, in opposition to the Word of God, is most irrelevant, especially because it would keep in darkness those who were supposed to be enlightened by it. Remember that Jesus, the Christ, had a prior existence as a Spirit, completely God in essence and in character before His advent on earth. In His prior existence, He was all divine, every bit as God the Father and the Holy Spirit. The three personalities of the Godhead always existed as One and will forever remain One for all eternity. But for the purposes of redemption, the council of heaven comprised of the Father, the Son, and the Holy Spirit, determined that the Son would invade the earthly realm and take upon Him the form of a man for the purpose of redemption and salvation of mankind.

Obviously, the work of redemption could not be accomplished in the physical world through a spirit, not possessing flesh and blood. An "earthly suit" was required to do the things necessary on earth for redemption and salvation. The purpose was to appease the heart of God, whose holiness could no longer endure the recurring animal sacrifices for the recurring sinful proclivity of humanity. Suffering is a tool in the hands of God to advance His revelation of love to humanity. Without equivocation, God endured suffering when Lucifer, the chief of the angels, rebelled against Him soon after creation. He further endured suffering when Israel and Judah, along with their various kings, rebelled against Him. Therefore, God who understands the virtue of suffering, searched for one in His Kingdom to satisfy the letter and the spirit of the law, but He could find none. Jesus was the sinless God-man, the only One qualified for the cross. This sacrifice would produce sons and daughters for God, after Jesus' excruciating experience on the cross. Jesus was and is the Suffering servant of God and is it any wonder that the apostle Paul shares similar experiences as one of the eminent servants of God. Evidently, the Son of God, Jesus, was set up to endure the humiliations of sinners: the very ones who, in their rush judgment, crucified the king of glory. The prophet Isaiah summed it up this way: "Yet it pleased the Lord to bruise Him, He has put him to grief" (Isa.53:10). Why, you ask? According to the book of Colossians, the apostle Paul, being a follower of Jesus, was unabashed about his sufferings when he said, "I now rejoice in my sufferings for you, and fill up in my flesh what is lacking in the afflictions of Christ, for the sake of His body, which is the church, of which I became a minister according to the stewardship from God which was given to me for you, for me to fulfill the word of God" (Col.1:24-25). Suffering is an essential quality of Christ likeness but defeat is not, unequivocally not. Paul's statement must not be understood to mean that the sufferings of Jesus, the Christ, was in any way deficient of the merits and requirements of redemption, but rather a progression in the whole idea of Man (Jesus) becoming God to mankind. In other words, God alone determines how each son or daughter would bring Him the most glory.

Leviticus 17:11 reminds us, "for it is the blood that makes atonement for the soul." This statement was further amplified in the New Testament: "And according to the law [the law of God], all things are purified by the blood and without the shedding of blood there is no remission" (Heb.9:22). This is the law of God as determined by the council of heaven, prior to the creation of the world, and the sin of Adam. Consistent with the goodness of God, the book of wisdom affirmed: "In mercy and truth, atonement is provided for iniquity." Whose iniquity? Atonement is provided for the iniquity of man (Prov. 16:6). God's nature is antithetical to the nature of Satan. This is why God is God. God's nature is love and that love is devoted to, surprisingly man, according to John 3:16. Love whatever you must, the priority is to love God and your neighbor, and anything else is secondary.

Jesus, the Man of Galilee, is the example of the "new thing" which God began to do throughout the entire universe, even today. Jesus is the epitome of the concept: the *new* man created according to God, in true righteousness and holiness (Eph.4:24). As far as Jesus is concerned, God would require nothing from us that He did not first accomplish in His Son. This is why it is important for all who come into the Kingdom of God, and seek to engage in the same mission as the Son of God, must know that Jesus is the only acceptable example to follow. Beyond the nobility of admiring and emulating great men and women of God (of our times), Jesus alone remains God's yardstick for growth and maturity for all believers. The Messiah left His natural environment, which is in the spiritual realm, to accept residence on earth for the purpose of fulfilling the will of the Father, who also is the Father of all who would believe in Him through the gospel of His Son. Jesus was not born to Joseph and Mary as Christ the Messiah, but as Jesus— the Savior of mankind. God became flesh through Jesus, and therefore, He dwells among us, even today.

Now, for humans to be born again, it must be a supernatural thing. Unfortunately, in much of the church world, including born-again and spirit-filled churches, the reason why Jesus commanded that one must be born again in order to see and to enter the Kingdom of God, are yet to be made clear. This is a supernatural thing, not based on whether man is tired of sin or not. According to the gospel of John, it is noted that "[we] were born [again], not of blood, nor of the will of the flesh, nor of the will of man, but of God" (Jn.1:13). To be born of God means that one is born for God and His Kingdom, at the moment of salvation and for all eternity. New believers in Jesus Christ are the descendants of God Himself, by faith, not merely descendants of Abraham according to the flesh. Nicodemus, in his innocent consternation about the subject of being "born again," harped on the statement by Jesus and wondered how a man, having been born into this world, could be born again a second time. As the Christ of God came into the world, not as spirit but of flesh and blood, so too, shall we become born again into the family of God, in heaven as spirit beings, through faith in God. We, the born-again and spirit-filled believers, must acknowledge that we were born out of a struggle for domination between the forces of darkness and the forces of Light. The struggle continues with us until His kingdom comes. The same war which Jesus fought for the souls of humanity still persists. This makes believers after Him "enlistees" of the war over the souls of men and women, those who are yet to come into the Kingdom of God. The purpose of Christian intercession, witnessing and evangelism is about the saving of the souls of men and women. Sons and daughters of God are equipped to do it in their own unique ways, to bring and nurture people for God. It takes faith in God to begin this new walk with Him, and to remain triumphant in it until the work on earth is done. The Spirit of Christ will not leave the Christian—the church—until the work on earth is complete.

The Scripture tells us that our true citizenship is in heaven. The part of human existence which is born again is the spirit of man, which represents divinity in man, the very image and likeness of God in humanity. Undoubtedly, the apostle Peter, looking ahead, provided further assurance to the born-again church that this is how Christians would become partakers of the divine nature of God, "having been born again, not of corruptible seed but incorruptible, through the Word of God which lives and abides forever" (1 Pet.1:23 and 2 Pet.1:4). The mystery of the Messiah, which the apostle Paul refers to as, "Christ in you, the hope of glory" (Col. 1:27), is the source of strength for the transformation of believers. He is the source of power to overcome the enemies of God and His Kingdom, in this life and in the one to come.

Christianity is war, whether or not one agrees. However, it is a different kind of war, not fought in the flesh or by means of worldly weapons, but by love through faith, 2 Corinthians 10:3-5 says, "For though we walk in the flesh, we do not war according to the flesh. For the weapons of our warfare are not carnal, but mighty in God for pulling down strongholds, casting down arguments and every high thing that exalts itself against the knowledge of God, bringing every thought into captivity to the obedience of Christ." Why? Because God is love, and love conquers all. Anyone who is born of love overcomes the world (1 Jn. 5:4).

Denominational churches have slobbered over the subject of salvation, and continue to do so, on the basis of what they consider their church traditions. The church of the Firstborn, the born-again and spirit-filled sons and daughters of God, must courageously teach and affirm the Word of God, which endures forever. The foregoing information, I am convinced, is at the heart of the mystery of new birth, which, to us, is no longer a mystery because God has revealed His will to mankind by His Spirit, who now resides in us. God has predestined us to be conformed to the image of His Son (Rom.8:29). God gives nothing to the Son which He will not offer to His sons and daughters, members of the church of the Firstborn. God does not envision defeat for His church and we must be careful not to perceive some of the betrayals in our lives as defeat, and so give Satan the victory, rather we must stand our ground and discover what God is up to. "For He does not afflict willingly, nor grieve the children of men" (Lam. 3:33). He is usually up to something!

Though Judas betrayed Jesus for 30 silver coins, afterwards, he had no appetite to enjoy what initially enticed him to betray the Son of God. Unfortunately, he lost his apostleship as a result. The case of Judas must be highlighted for all believers not to be obsessed with material gains and eventually forfeit one's place in the Kingdom of God. The nature of evil does not cease when one is born-again, but the difference is that the born-again and spirit-filled child of God is given total and complete access to God, through the Holy Spirit, to appropriate the graces of God, to fend off the attacks of demons, and stand triumphant before God. Being born-again and spirit-filled makes one a conqueror over Satan, just like God the Son was and ever shall be.

I woke up one morning for the start of my quiet time and the Spirit of God spoke, as clearly as it could be audibly perceived by the ear, but in the spirit. He said, "God is up to something." Without any thought to it, or hesitation, I responded: "I am ever so ready." That happened years ago. And now, the truth is that God is still up to something, and my response will ever be, "I am ever so ready."

Chapter Four

The Miracle of Salvation

Why is salvation a miracle? Because the journey of a relationship with God in His almightiness, holiness, righteousness, and the list goes on, begins with being born-again into the family of God, where Jesus is the first born. This is an inescapable experience for those who wish to become sons and daughters of God after Jesus Christ, and it cannot be circumvented. The Son of God was conceived in the womb of Mary when the angel Gabriel appeared and greeted the Virgin Mary in this manner: "Rejoice highly favored one, the Lord is with you, blessed are you among women!" But when she saw him, she was troubled at the saying, and considered what manner of greeting this was. Then the angel said to her, "Do not be afraid, Mary, for you have found favor with God. And behold, you shall conceive in your womb and bring forth a Son, and shall call His name Jesus" (Lk.1:28-31). The message from God which the angel, Gabriel, took to Joseph and his wife, Mary, was the Word of God. It was the agent of conception for the child Jesus in the womb of His mother. So Mary conceived a Son, Jesus, by the Word of God, enabled by the power of the Holy Spirit.

Similarly, a Christian believer, is born again into the family of God by means of the Word of God – the incorruptible seed of the Word of God (Jn.1:13 and 1 Pet.1:23), enabled by the power of the Holy Spirit. In case the aforementioned Scriptures are not enough, listen to the words of James (Jesus' earthly brother): "Of His own will He brought us forth by the word of truth, that we might be a kind of first-fruits of His creatures" (James 1:18). All references point to God bringing us into His Kingdom, as though from the womb of God and that womb of God is His word. This is similar to the womb of Mary, from where Jesus was born into the world. The birth of Jesus on earth was a spiritual event. It was a thing of great joy for the inhabitants of the earth, and so is the event of the birth of a child of God in heaven. It means they have repented from their sins, which causes great rejoicing for the angels of God in heaven (Lk.2:13 and 15:7). Angels and humans celebrated the birth of Jesus on earth. In heaven, the angels and saints celebrate the birth of a child of God into His Kingdom, those who repent of their sins. It is the love and grace of God toward humanity that produced both events, in heaven and upon the earth. So, when Jesus said, "You must be born again…" it was a command similar to every other thing the Christian is commanded to do. Every word of God is a command and a command, by its nature, is not subject to review, but must be obeyed. It is a non-negotiable command that has no substitute.

Back again to the holy encounter between Jesus and Nicodemus, Jesus said: "Most assuredly I say to you, unless a man is born again, he cannot see the kingdom of God." Now notice that the initial, or the first experience, of being born again is to see the Kingdom of God. This means that although the Kingdom of God is upon us, it is still invisible to the natural eyes of humanity, those who are preoccupied with the dictates of living according to the flesh. It is a wise and noble thing to engage in the activity of genuine living, if that activity of living does not take the place of God. God desires fellowship with man because He created him for that very reason. If all that a man knows and sees is his little profession of making a living that is a very sad existence.

Consider for a moment how the Lord Jesus responded to the conversation of the two disciples on their journey from Jerusalem to Emmaus found in Luke 24:17-25. The two were discussing the events of the burial and the resurrection of Jesus. Jesus said, "What kind of conversation is this that you have with one another as you walk and are sad?" One of the two disciples, with a voice of irritation, questioned Jesus and asked, "Are you the only stranger in Jerusalem, and have you not known the things which happened there in these days?" And the Lord, with a little exasperation in His voice, said: "O foolish ones, and slow of heart to believe in all that the prophets have spoken! Ought not the Christ to have suffered these things and to enter His glory" (Lk.24:18, 25, 31). The scripture went on to say in verse 31: "Then, their eyes were opened and they knew Him, and He vanished from their sight". Obviously, the disciples were not blind physically, but the very fact that they lacked the wisdom to connect the story of the events in Jerusalem with the prophetic words of the Scripture, especially being disciples who attended some of Jesus' meetings, confirms their spiritual blindness. Otherwise, why open the eyes of men who had clear vision? Was it not to perceive spiritual truth? So the mind, too, can be an agent of "sight" beyond imagining things.

Clearly, someone who is not in Christ, whose sins and iniquities have not been forgiven by the blood of Jesus and by the washing of the water of regeneration, cannot see the benefit of living for God in his or her sinful state of mind. The Kingdom of God is there, but he is incapable of perceiving it because spiritual things cannot be perceived by carnal minds. Christianity is 100% spiritual and it is all the work of the Holy Spirit. Christianity is a walk of faith in the spirit. Man cannot rest on his natural senses alone to accomplish anything worthwhile for the Kingdom of God, "For we walk by faith and not by sight" (2 Cor.5:7). When Jesus announced the platform of His ministry in Luke 4:18, one aspect of His platform was to give recovery of sight to the blind. I am convinced that blindness in that context and section of the Scripture is not limited to the disease of physical blindness, but even more so—spiritual blindness. Spiritual blindness appears to be a major malady, more than physical blindness which could be corrected medically or through a miracle from God, because it keeps people away from the Kingdom of God. Jesus told the Pharisees in the book of John (9:41), that it would have been better for them if they had been blind so that He could have healed them, but because they claimed that they could see (and were not sinners of the Gentile sort), they would remain blind and die in their sin. Their spiritual blindness was a major reason for their rebellion against the Lord, which further complicated their ability to appreciate and comprehend the truth of His teachings.

Another case in point: Consider the salvation of the apostle Paul. He was a Pharisee who probably knew the Torah from cover to cover or, at the least, and quite obviously had sufficient knowledge of the Torah to be able to teach others. He was a leader among the Pharisees. He was the one who consented to the death of Stephen, a disciple of Jesus. When he went back to the Sanhedrin in Jerusalem and obtained papers to travel to Damascus to arrest believers in that city, he was struck by a shimmering light, and he immediately became blind. The man, Saul of Tarsus, was about to come face-to-face with His Lord and discover his destiny in an unusual way and dramatic fashion. He had been blind in truth and the reality of matters pertaining to the Kingdom of God. The same blindness which caused him to be enraged by the truth of the gospel, at that moment manifested as a true physical ailment and the man needed a healer. That healer was, and still is, Jesus. This is what the Lord told Nicodemus as the initial experience of coming into the kingdom of God. Saul, the man of Tarsus, would not enter the Kingdom of God in his natural state and become a doer of the Word of God. He had to become blind to the world, so that when his sight was recovered, he would be able to truly see and understand spiritual things. Thus, the prophet Ananias was sent by the Holy Spirit to meet Saul and lay hands over his eyes, so that Paul would receive his first miracle—the removal of his *blindness* in the things of the Kingdom of God.

To provide further illustration, let's consider the writings of the man of Tarsus himself. His name, of necessity, being changed from Saul to Paul, he writes in his epistle to the Romans: "For I do not desire, brethren, that you should be ignorant of this mystery, lest you should be wise in your own opinion, that blindness in part has happened to Israel until the fullness of the Gentiles has come" (Rom.11:25). It is the same language which Jesus used to depict the Pharisees and, unfortunately, the Jewish public at large, as "blind leaders of the blind" (Matt. 15:14). The gospel of the Kingdom of God is foolishness to the world, but eternal, abundant life, and peace to believers. The devil's ultimate goal is to hinder and keep people away from hearing the gospel, and so lead them to miss the opportunity to enter heaven.

In another section of his writings, the apostle Paul identified the culprit behind the lack of receptivity to the gospel: "But even if our gospel is veiled, it is veiled to those who are perishing, whose minds the god of this age has blinded, who do not believe, lest the light of the gospel of the glory of Christ, who is the image of God should shine on them" (2 Cor. 4:4). This salvation comes to us when we, by faith, confess the Word of God with our mouths and believe in our hearts that Jesus died on the cross of Cavalry, was buried, and raised again from the dead for our justification. At that point, the miracle occurs when the Holy Spirit lifts the scales from our eyes and we are able to acknowledge the limitations of the temporal world, and so embrace the Kingdom of God and the unlimited resources of heaven. It is a free gift of God by His grace.

What is Salvation? Salvation is the message of redemption for mankind from sin. The Son of God was given His name "Jesus" specifically for the work that He was born to do as God in the flesh. Humanity is lost in sin and iniquity and, therefore, needs a Savior. The blood of animals from the Old Covenant was not sufficient to make one righteous. The sacrifice of a sinless and holy being was the only acceptable thing to appease the heart of a Holy God, once and for all, and remove the obstacle of sin and iniquity. And the Lord Himself summed it up when He said, "For the Son of Man has come to seek and to save that which is lost" (Lk.19:10). This Jesus is the Lamb of God, the only acceptable sacrifice and offering for sinners which meets every ordinance and requirement of the Law for the salvation of mankind. The apostle Peter speaking before the Sanhedrin, the Jewish religious authority of his time, most emphatically stated, "This is the stone which was rejected by you builders, which has become the chief cornerstone. Nor is there salvation in any other, for there is no name under heaven given among men by which we must be saved" (Acts 4:11-12). This is the undisputed evidence, or testimony, from the Scripture that religion is a hassle and brings about weariness to the spirit, soul, and body. Only Jesus, and Him alone, is the answer to all the cries of the heart of man, Jew or Gentile (non-Jew).

Salvation is a total package deal. Biblically speaking, when one is saved it includes eternal life (going to heaven when one dies), healing, preservation, deliverance, happiness, prosperity and soundness of mind. The entire gift could be received once, or in a progressive manner. The admonition is to live it out daily. This is the covenant the Son of God offers to everyone who seeks fellowship with God through Himself. And, I think it is a mighty big deal! Now, one might wonder what salvation is truly about, in light of the problem of lack, poverty, sin, and sickness among believers. Why are some believers in Christ living out the promises of God while others are not? To answer the question, it is necessary to point out that there are men and women all over the world, born-again and spirit-filled believers, who are presently living and breathing the abundance of salvation. All the promises of God are for the "whosoever," those who embrace the Word of God, who qualify to partake in the unhindered access to His grace. Again, it is personal, a *whosoever* thing, and who knows, if you are that *whosoever* when you present yourself before God to enjoy the life which God has promised. The apostle Paul said, "Indeed, let God be true and every man a liar" (Rom.3:4). God will uphold His side of the bargain, if we will uphold our side of the bargain. Furthermore, the Scripture adds: "Therefore, it is of faith that it might be according to grace, so that the promises of God might be sure to all the seed, not only to those who are of the law, but also to those who are of the faith of Abraham, who is the father of us all" (Rom.4:16).

Two Kinds of Baptisms

There are two distinct baptisms mentioned in the Scripture. The first one is water baptism, which characterized much of John the Baptist's ministry. The other refers to the baptism of the Holy Spirit. Quite often, being filled with the Holy Spirit can also be said to be, being baptized in the Holy Spirit. For that reason, I will endeavor in the same prologue of discussing the baptism of the Holy Spirit to say a few things about the first baptism, which is as much a cardinal doctrine of the Christian church as being filled by the Holy Spirit.

Water baptism is a physical event which has great spiritual implication and symbolism. Blood, Light (Fire) and Water are three natural elements, which have as much significance in the physical realm as in the spiritual domain. These three elements have both physical and spiritual relevance in the history of mankind. They are just as ubiquitous in the redemption and salvation of mankind. In Exodus 40:30-32, God instructed Moses, the leader of the first congregation of God, to set a laver of water between the tent of the congregation and the altar, where Moses and the priests of the congregation would wash their hands and feet for cleansing and purification before they would approach God. Although, the cleansing process assumed a mere symbolic significance, the act was much deeper than that. The temple of God and all the other articles of the temple were sacred and dedicated objects for use only in the act of praise and worship of God.

Water, in that respect, had a powerful symbolism, both as a cleansing agent in the natural, and also as a deeper spiritual agent for purification of the heart. The apostle Paul described the experience when Moses led Israel through the Red Sea and said: "our fathers were under the cloud, and all passed through the sea, all ate the same spiritual food, and all drank the same spiritual drink" (1 Cor. 10:1-4) as a form of baptism. Baptism unto Moses was merely an allusion to the wilderness experience, of which Moses was the leader of the congregation (See Exodus 14 and 1 Cor. 10). Another significant testimony on the subject of water baptism is from the apostle Peter. He described how Noah, a preacher of righteousness, saved eight souls. He used the water of Noah as a form of baptism, "not for the removal of the filth of the flesh, but an answer of a good conscience toward God, through the resurrection of Jesus Christ" (1 Pet. 3: 20 -21).

The Ministry of John the Baptist

The prophet Malachi testified about the ministry of John the Baptist in this manner: "Remember the Law of Moses which I commanded him in Horeb for all Israel, with the statutes and judgments. Behold the coming of the great and dreadful day of the Lord. And he will turn the hearts of the fathers to the children, and the hearts of the children to their fathers, lest I come and strike the earth with a curse" (Mal.3:4-6). The ministry of John the Baptist had an unusual nature in that he did not come looking for people to be converted. Instead, the people came looking for him and even when they found him, he was not particularly amenable to their spiritual depravity, especially to the religious people of his day, but forthrightly chastened them for their empty religiousness. Moreover, his preaching was in the wilderness, and close to the Jordan River where he administered water baptism to those who believed his preaching who repented of their sins. But when the Son of God approached John to be baptized by him, he instinctively pushed back and said to the Lord, "I need to be baptized by You and are You coming to me?"(Matt. 3:14). Now, consider the answer of Jesus, "Permit it to be so now, for thus it is fitting for us to fulfill all righteousness" (Matt. 3:15).

Baptism to fulfill all righteousness! Yes indeed, because John had a need to be baptized by the Lord, but not the other way around. Nevertheless, the Father requires nothing of His children which He did not first accomplish in His only begotten Son. So, baptism becomes a major doctrine of the Christian church, which it administers publicly for those who profess faith in Jesus, our Lord and Savior. The purpose of Jesus' baptism was not repentance from sin, but that He would partake of the experience that He would later expect of His followers. Also, it was to fulfill all the Law and ordinances of Moses. Jesus had no sin to repent of because, as John G. Lake said, "Christ is at once the spotless descent of God into men (man), and sinless ascent of man into God." He is the Holy Lamb of God who took away the sin of the world. He has no sin in His soul or in His flesh to be repented of, and consequently, does not need to be baptized, but He was baptized by emersion in the water of the Jordan, to fulfill all righteousness. His was a life marked by unquestioned obedience to every precept of the word of God. Again, God would have nothing for the Son which He would not require from sons and daughters of God after Him. Therefore, water baptism is required of all believers who are born-again and filled with the Holy Spirit of God. It is an outward affirmation of a lifestyle of obedience to the Son of God, who gave us the right to be called sons and daughters of God. It is not enough to be children and perpetually wallow in childishness. It is not right to accept one aspect of the teaching and seek to argue one's way through the other, simply because someone, somewhere, made a derogatory, unintelligent statement about something they do not particularly like or understand about the gifts of God. We must grow up and become mature in the business of the Kingdom, and that is what the message of sons and daughters of God is intended to convey to the church and to Christians all over the world.

One of the best courses in my graduate classes at a Christian university was, Progress of Redemption. The Spirit of God is a master organizer, and scheduler of events and He does not begin to establish His work in the life of His children in a haphazard fashion. He is deliberately meticulous to ensure that there is provision for every need, by His grace, for the journey ahead of those who are called to witness for Him. He is immaculately methodical and gentle, too, in all of His dealings with humanity and, of course, His sons and daughters. One must first begin to look at things from a Kingdom perspective, in order to participate actively in the business of the Kingdom. It is never enough to get saved, join a church, and become a missionary without a proper understanding of the role of the Holy Spirit. Revelation increases as one grows in the knowledge of God, through His Word. Growth and maturity in Christianity is a daily experience, which is ill-afforded to those who are too busy and preoccupied with the business of living and forget the author of life. Ironically, this is a church issue and not one for the un-churched, but by no means exonerates the unchurched from their rebellion against the Son of God.

Rebellion against the Son of God persists because humans operate in the physical and temporal plane. *Sight*, in the Kingdom of God, is accomplished when man accepts the Lordship of Jesus—the Christ, and surrenders to His will. Thereafter, ignorance is revealed and the allures of this world are dealt with, and one begins to perceive with the heart and understand with the mind the things that matter in this life and the one to come. God is eternally focused on the Christian mission to bring souls into His Kingdom and this must remain the focus of the church. Remember, this universe is an ordered universe, irrespective of satanic opposition toward God and His followers. We must not forget that the end of Satan has been determined and he is incapable of redemption (even if it were offered to him). His place, at the bottom of the lake, which burns with unquenchable fire, where the worms live forever, is dead-set and there is nothing he can do but to burn forever.

The Holy Spirit of God is the agent through whom we enter into the Kingdom of God and begin to actively participate in the business of the Kingdom of God. He alone empowers, equips, trains, instructs, guides and leads believers to do the will of the Father. Especially, as He is the God in the church contemporary, who represents the Lord Jesus—the Christ and the Father. He is the gift of the Father to the church of the Firstborn. He was with Jesus, the Christ, during His earthly ministry and He is with all believers who are witnesses for the Lord today. God the Father will give nothing to the Son which He would not give to us. Once again, the Holy Spirit is God's proffered gift to His church. Forget your religious ideas about who or what the Holy Spirit is about. Spookiness is of the devil. The Holy Spirit is holy. He is God in every sense of the word. We receive Him, by faith, just as we receive Jesus Christ at the moment of salvation. Follow the Scripture and do what it says.

Above all, we will be walking in disobedience when we accept one part of the teaching and command of Jesus the Christ, and reject the other, due to something someone said ignorantly about other aspects of Scripture. Read John 3: 3-5, as a unit of thought, and you will gain fresh insight. The Holy Spirit is our able companion, whose presence and power are sufficient for every ministry need. He is to be received by faith, not by the desire of some minister attempting to push us down and/or compel us to participate in an all-night prayer to receive the Holy Spirit when we do not even know what it means to pray. The church of Jesus Christ, not of the religious "latter day saints" is for the past and present day saints (Old and New Testament believers), and so belong to the Holy Spirit. Sons and daughters of God cannot afford not to be filled with His presence and power. It is impossible for the Christian to function in the ministry of Jesus Christ without the help of the Holy Spirit.

Going back to my Progress of Redemption class, it provided me with a crystal clear picture, with biblical illustrations, of how the revelation of God increases from generation to generation. It was in that class that the professor made a statement unheard of, at least by me, that the only way to estimate the value of a man's soul is to compare it to the value of the

One who offered His life to die in his stead. Up until that moment, process theology was confusing and unimpressive chatter. Thereafter, Scripture appears logical, reasonable, and very relevant for the existence of life on earth, with respect to biblical history and God's ideal of life. The invisible hand of God becomes all the more visible as humanity moves from one stage of affair to the other. God's revelation through nature and Scripture, seem harmonious and complementary to each other but never at odds. Revelation is calibrated and dispensed according to the capacity of each individual to honor the Giver, and to walk according to the dictates of Scripture, led by the Holy Spirit. The way God dealt with Adam in the Garden of Eden was markedly different from the way He dealt with Noah before, and after, the flood. He referred to Abraham as His Friend, but honored Isaac and Jacob as direct descendants of His friend, Abraham. He visited the least of the patriarchs Joseph in dreams, and strengthened him to overcome adversities. He did this to preserve a people for Himself, who would be delivered from the bondage of slavery, and eventually possess the Promised Land. From exodus— through captivity into the hands of foreign oppressors— the invisible hand of God continually guided the nation of Israel through moments of relative peace, rebellion, punishment and redemption. He never, completely, abandoned them into the hands of their enemies. Man cannot afford a life without the revelation of God. His Word is the anchor that holds the universe. Jesus is both the Living and Written Word of God. Let's read what the apostle Paul said about the indispensability of God's Word (The Living Lord) over humanity: "Therefore God also has highly exalted Him and given Him the name which is above every name, that at the name of Jesus, every knee should bow, of those in heaven, and of those on earth, and of those under the earth, and that every tongue should confess that Jesus Christ is Lord to the glory of God the Father" (Phil. 2:9-11). Jesus alone saves, heals, delivers and baptizes in the Holy Spirit.

Jesus Christ describes the Holy Spirit as "the Promise of the Father" to His children, *all* His children. The beloved physician Luke, by the same inspiration, provides us with theological insight about the essential nature of a spirit-filled and spirit-led life, a prerequisite for all disciples who would venture to labor in the Spirit of Christ for the salvation of the lost. "Behold,

I send the Promise of My Father upon you but tarry in the city of Jerusalem until you are endued with power from on high" (Lk.24:49). It is the Holy Spirit who gives us power for ministry. Call it grace, call it anointing, it is one and the same, and every believer must operate in Christ and through Him, to flow in His grace and anointing. Remember, the attempt here is to point to what the Scripture says on the subject. Some have been involved in the ministry for years and still deny Him His rightful place in guiding and directing ministry activities. Let it be clear, those who engage in ministry without being spirit-filled and spirit directed, do so at their own volition. Frustration and unfruitfulness are the consequences of a ministry without the operation of the Holy Spirit in the Kingdom of God.

In another portion of the Scripture, we read: "He said to them, it is not for you to know times or seasons which the Father has put in His own authority, but you will receive power when the Holy Spirit has come upon you and you shall be witnesses to Me in Jerusalem, and in Judea, and Samaria, and to the end of the earth" (Acts 1:7-8). Believers pray to be filled with the Holy Spirit because He is the power and wisdom of God for the ministry of the Kingdom of God. He is presently the One who leads, directs, and orchestrates the moves of God in the church, as well as in the lives of believers, to the glory of the Father and the Son. Whether you call it baptism of the Holy Spirit, baptism in the Holy Spirit, or baptism with the Holy Spirit, they are one and the same. The important thing is that one is "baptized in," "baptized of," or "baptized with" the Holy Spirit. The result, by the grace of God, is a ministry that operates in the demonstration of the power of God, to save, heal, and deliver those oppressed by Satan. The subject and substance of a spirit-filled life is about possessing the power of God to minister, preach, teach, heal, deliver, pray, cast out demons, and any other thing ministers do that is in accordance with sound doctrine. To be filled with the Spirit means that one is undeniably dependent upon Him for the orchestrations and outcomes of ministry. We work for Him and with Him, and in a most pleasant twist, He works with us, yet we are accountable to Him. He is not accountable to us. My point is that God Almighty desires to live His life through us, to enable us fulfill His will for us now and forever.

Hopefully, the case has been made to portray the Holy Spirit as the God of the church age, with all the attributes of Omnipotence, Omnipresence and Omniscience just like the Father and the Son. Therefore, let us consider the gifts of the Spirit and most specifically, the gift of tongues, which engenders much of the debate about the Holy Spirit. There are on the whole nine gifts of the spirit recorded in the bible, and if by any means of evaluation, some of the gifts are cherished as from God, while others are considered 'somewhat' of an alternate source, one must let the bible speak for itself in order to discern the truth. In 1 Cor.12: 8-10, the following gifts are listed: the word of wisdom, word of knowledge, faith, gifts of healings, working of miracles, prophesy, discerning of spirits, diversity of tongues, and interpretation of tongues. Apparently, much of the furor on the use and applications of the gifts of the Spirit emanate from the last two about tongues and interpretations, and only God knows why. It ought not to be so, but it is. According to the Bible "Every good and every perfect gift is from above, and comes down from the Father of lights, with whom there is no variation or shadow of turning" (James 1:17). True biblical admonition is to "covet the best gifts" but not to reject any gift. If, and when we reject any gift of God due to false doctrine or ignorance, we flagrantly dishonor God and His Word. Being filled with the Spirit does not guarantee anyone a life free from temptation or tribulation. However, His presence empowers believers to resist demonic activities or even cast demons out and stop the oppression. Desire the gift and pray the prayer of faith and the gift will be given. It could happen by the laying of hands from the minister or ministers, or by simply praying the prayer of faith.

Chapter Five

Sons and Daughters of God

In the words of Solomon, the wisest man that ever lived, "let us hear the conclusion of the whole matter" of creation, redemption and resurrection of life as witnessed by the Holy Scripture. The Son of God—Jesus—is both the symbol and the substance of the Holy Scripture and of Christianity. Evidently, He represents the cusp of Christianity, and the church's relationship with God. The phrase "sons and daughters of God" is a contemporary expression of a similar phrase employed in Genesis six "sons of God," which has interpretive difficulties because biblical scholars were, and still are, unsure if the term was a direct reference to the sons of Adam, or a reference to angelic hosts of heaven, or simply a combination of both. But that is not the case in the New Testament in terms of usage.

Just as it was said of Jesus Christ: "You are a priest forever according to the order of Melchizedek" (Heb.7:17), sons and daughters of God are forever so after the order of Jesus Christ. Jesus Christ is the first and only begotten Son of God, and through Him believers in God become sons and daughters of God, ultimately in that order. It is vitally important for every believer to comprehend the spiritual and historical significance of his or her relationship with God through Jesus, the Son of God.

When Jesus spoke about the greatness of His cousin, John the Baptist, His disciples felt as though He did not mean what He had just said to them. The statement may have sounded so preposterous to them, yet they never bothered to privately, or publicly, inquire of Him what He meant. They were not careful to ask Him what He meant by declaring John the Baptist the greatest of all prophets who came before him. Our contemporary saints, singers, worshippers and instrumentalists in sacred music remind us that Christianity is all about Jesus, and that the Messiah—the Christ of God—is the measure of the man (believer). Again, the truth is that Jesus meant every bit of what the disciples had heard from Him. In Matthew 11:11, Jesus said: "Assuredly, I say to you, among those born of women, there has not risen one greater than John the Baptist; but he who is least in the Kingdom of heaven is greater than he." Jesus must not be serious, His disciples may have quibbled. After all, Moses had face-to-face meetings with God. How could John the Baptist, who never saw God face-to-face, actually be greater than Moses?

What about Elijah, the man of God who could call down fire from heaven or bring rain from heaven upon the earth? Is John the Baptist greater than he? What of Isaiah, Jeremiah, Ezekiel, Daniel, just to name but a few? How could John the Baptist be greater than all of them? What great miracle did John the Baptist perform that distinguished him from the rest of the prophets of the Old Testament and/or what book of the Bible did he write with revelations greater than those written by the other prophets? The Psalmist David and the apostle Paul both concur that Jesus is God's proffered gift to humanity. He is the beginning of the new specimen of the children of God, and better yet, He is the absolute prototype of a class of humans, who embody God both in form and fashion. John the Beloved was ecstatic and full of faith when he declared to us, "as He is so are we in this world" (1 John 4:17), and this declaration does not make anything easy for the Christian, but rather supports the fact that Christianity is essentially spiritual, and shall ever remain an unconquerable force on earth and beyond. "For with God all things are possible" (Mk. 10:27), the God of the Christian.

In case you have not yet noticed, Only God can say anything He wishes to say and be right about it. No other being can do that, and that is what separates God from any other being. He is the Omnipotent, Omnipresent, and Omniscient One. Let the wonder continue as we prostrate ourselves and worship Him because there is none like Him. John the Baptist was conceived in the womb of his mother, Elizabeth, after the natural order of mating between a husband and a wife. She had been barren for several years.

Although the conception and birth of John the Baptist was a great miracle, he was nevertheless, born in sin. His conception was not an immaculate conception, according to Roman Catholic doctrine. However, Jesus was conceived in the womb of the Virgin Mary as the Word of God, a true immaculate conception, which eventually became flesh, and dwelt among us. Joseph, Jesus' earthly father, had nothing to do with the process. Now, consider sons and daughters of God after Jesus. It is recorded in Scripture that "we were born, [again] not of blood, nor of the will of the flesh," as in case of John the Baptist, "nor of the will of man; but of God" (Jn.1:13). John the Baptist became the greatest of all the old prophets because to him alone was given the honor to see, touch, and introduce the very One whom all the prophets before Him had enquired, prophesied and written about. Until today, there is absolutely nothing since the history of creation that could compare with the coming of Jesus, the God-Man, into the world. Jesus is the answer to everything which ails humanity. John the Baptist was given the distinct honor to introduce Him to all of mankind, and that is very special.

The Significance of Sons and Daughters of God

Naturally speaking, authority and responsibility represent both sides of the same coin. Authority without responsibility produces tyranny, and responsibility without authority equals broken promises. While nature abhors tyranny and broken promises, the church must not simply approve the way of nature, but rise above it to demonstrate a better way. It is not simply one or the other. Jesus has entrusted both authority and responsibility to sons and daughters of God to do business in the Kingdom until He returns. Authority and responsibility are necessary in order to conduct business in the Kingdom of God, on behalf of the Father, the Son, and the Holy Spirit. Sons and daughters of God have authority and responsibility in the Kingdom of God to represent Him. That is true balance. Jesus, the first born Son of God, is the classic example of the privilege of power and the responsibility that goes with it. Our conformity to His image must correspond to His full obedience and demonstration of the power of God, relative to His very platform of ministry as recorded in Luke 4: 18-19. The beloved physician Luke further alluded to the "things" which Jesus "began both to do and to teach" in chapter 24:19 and in Acts 1:1, in conformity with the earlier passage of Lk.4:18-19, which ought to be the sum total of the ministry of the church. Our conformity to the image of Jesus the Christ means that we must use the power given to us to serve God in His Kingdom. Sons and daughters of God are born again and spirit filled believers according to Jn.1.13 and 1Pet.1:23. This is one distinction a true believer, born-again, and spirit-filled Christian shares with the Lord Jesus. Upon further elaboration, the Scripture describes Christians or believers as members of the "general assembly and church of the Firstborn [Jesus] who are registered in heaven" (Heb.12:23). Additionally, Romans 8:29 speaks of Jesus as the "Firstborn among many brethren, of whom we are," and the apostle Paul was unhinged when he declared Him as "…the image of the invisible God, the Firstborn over all creation, His Lordship not limited to believers alone but also to unbelievers." Jesus was, and is, the Firstborn Son of God, as recorded both in heaven and on earth. And next are the ones who follow after Him, those who accept the Word of God in John 3: 3-5, "who have become sons and daughters of God through Him." In the prior dispensation, God spoke to His prophets and priests by His Word, but in the current dispensation, after Jesus, God lives in His sons and daughters, a life which is made a reality through the obedience of Jesus' death on the cross of Calvary, burial and resurrection from the dead.

Every other prophet before John Spoke about Jesus— the Christ of God—but to John alone was given the special privilege to see Him face-to-face, touch, and converse with Him (the very One who other prophets had spoken and written so much about, the Lord of all). He is the sum and substance of all revelation, "The testimony of Jesus is the spirit of prophesy" (Rev.19:10), and of whom, the scripture further declares: "Then I said, behold, I have come in the volume of the book it is written of Me to do Your will, O Lord." As earlier mentioned, Jesus is the "new thing," which God began to do with humanity. He is God in the flesh, something the world had never witnessed until His advent into the world. A world of limitations and all manner of sin, yet He was without sin. Also, the same Spirit who raised

Jesus from the dead dwells in every born-again and spirit-filled believer, irrespective of the silly and useless rancor over the person and the gifts of the Holy Spirit (especially tongues). Therefore, the strength of the believer is in the Son of God, "Christ in you, the hope of glory" (Col. 1:27), who grants to all equal access to the throne and presence of Almighty God just as the Son is with the Father."

Chapter Six

Spiritual Authority

In the realm of the spirit, the name of Jesus strikes fear upon hell and all its hierarchy. Hell trembles at the mention of His name. The demon-possessed man in Matthew 8:28-29, cried out: "what have we to do with You, Jesus, You Son of God? Have You come here to torment us before the time?" Although the religious community of His day did not recognize and acknowledge Him as the Christ of God, the demons obviously knew Him very well. They knew Him and acknowledged that whatever punishment He was about to exert on them, at that moment, was premature because they knew it was not yet time for the final punishment. Apparently, they were aware of the place of punishment reserved for Satan and all his cohorts. That is, the bottomless pit, which burns with unquenchable fire, whose worms never die. The name *Jesus* is not just the symbol and substance of Christianity, but the power upon which the church was founded.

In another section of the Bible, we are reminded of another event where the sons of a Jewish chief priest attempted to replicate the miracles of Jesus by calling on His name in the same manner they heard the apostle Paul. Here is the story: "Then some of the itinerant Jewish exorcists took it upon themselves to call the name of the Lord Jesus over those who had evil spirits, saying 'we exorcise you by the Jesus whom Paul preaches.' Also there were seven sons of Sceva, a Jewish chief priest who did so. And the evil spirit answered and said, 'Jesus I know, and Paul I know; but who are you?' And the man, in whom the evil spirit was leaped on them, overpowered them, so that they fled out of that house naked and wounded" (Acts19:13-16).

From the foregoing we can infer that all sons and daughters of God are descendants of Abraham, but not all sons and daughters of Abraham are sons and daughters of God. The distinction needs to be observed. Religion, indeed, mimics true Christianity, but it lacks the power and authority to accomplish the will of God. Sons and daughters of God obey the Word of God. When Jesus said, "You must be born again of water and the spirit" (Jn 3:5), He was not offering a suggestion. Like every word of God, it was, and still is, a command. The command is to repent (be born again) and to receive the gift of the Holy Spirit. Christianity, as we have previously established, demands a relationship with God and that is how it is done. The Holy Spirit is not promised to those who ignore and rebel against the command of Jesus Christ. Sons and daughters of God must be separated from the children of God. After all, humanity belongs to God until "all the Kingdoms of this world have become the Kingdoms of our Lord and His Christ where He reigns forever" (Rev.11:15), indicating that the work of redemption and salvation have come to a close. Until then, sons and daughters of God are needed to fulfill their assignments, to make disciples of all nations and rescue souls from destruction.

Chapter Seven

Spiritual Responsibility

Demons knew Paul the apostle, and without a doubt, knew Peter, John, James and the rest. Also Satan, and his angels, knew men and women of God such as, Smith Wigglesworth, John G. Lake, A. A. Allen, Jack Coe, Aimee Semple McPherson, Kathryn Cullman, Oral Roberts, Kenneth E. Haggin, Kenneth Copeland, Benny Hinn, and several others (both deceased and living), who have accomplished and are accomplishing great evangelistic work for the Kingdom of God, even as it is to this day. In Luke 10:19 Jesus said, "Behold I give you the authority to trample on serpents and scorpions and over all the power of the enemy, and nothing shall by any means hurt you." This power and authority to operate as Kingdom citizens is limited to those who obey the scripture. In Acts 16:16, a slave girl, who had a spirit of divination recognized Paul as one with authority in the spirit realm and called him out as a servant of the Most High God. While the owner of the slave girl, and the people in the community, acknowledged no such thing, the girl who operates with a familiar spirit recognized Paul. Above all, we have heard anecdotally, or perhaps witnessed incidents, where men and women who have no relationship with God through Jesus Christ, pretend to speak as Christians, attempt to do what Christians do, but were, unfortunately, destroyed by demon spirits. It is not about whether one is perfect or not. To be certain, no one is perfect before God. Only Jesus can make a man righteous and able to defeat demon spirits.

The phrase "no one perfect" is an evasive reaction of a sin-sick soul seeking to find solace from the degradation of sin, without confronting the sin nature of humanity. Jesus is the only perfect human able to appease the heart of God for the sin of the entire world. God will never demand holiness or perfection from a son or daughter of Adam, who is yet to surrender his or her will to the Lordship of Jesus Christ. It was no accident that Jesus died to redeem humanity from sin. Adam was created innocent, but not perfect as long as he retained the right to choose. Consequently, all descendants of Adam were born in sin and were, by their very nature, in need of a Savior. Therefore only those, who in obedience to the word of God, submit and embrace Jesus as their Lord and Savior, will have their sins forgiven. Humanity's longing for perfection and holiness will be bequeathed only to those who are in Christ. When God said, as far as the east is removed from the west, so far have I removed your sins from Me, He wasn't daring sinful men and women to test His resolve and capacity to save and to forgive, but He was. When He said you must be born again and be filled with the Spirit to enter His Kingdom, He was not attempting to highlight heaven as the ultimate experience for the believer, even though He was. However, He was emphatically reminding those who dare to believe and obey His word that they, too, can live joyfully and in peace and victoriously as the Son of God. They can demonstrate, through their own lives, the same grace and power that were available to the Son of God during His time on earth. Jesus is the One who baptizes believers in the Holy Spirit, who alone gives the gifts of ministry to His church.

The person of Jesus, the Man of Galilee, is the focal point of Christianity. No wonder the scripture describes Him as "a stumbling stone and a rock of offence," and, unfortunately, people are still stumbling and being offended by the very name who delivers humanity from the distresses of life and living. He is the beginning and the end of Christianity. According to the gospel of Matthew, the Lord chided the disciples not in a demeaning manner, but rather admonishing them as a privileged group, when He said: "Blessed are your eyes for they see, and your ears for they hear: for assuredly, I say to you that many prophets and righteous men desired to see what you see, and did not see it, and to hear what you hear, and did not hear it" (Matt.13:17). Simeon, one of the last of the Old Testament saints, lived the remainder of his life waiting for what he called "the Consolation of Israel" and after he had seen the Lord's Christ, "he took Him up in his arms and blessed God and said: Lord, now You are letting Your servant depart in peace according to Your word: for my eyes have seen Your salvation which You have prepared before the face of all peoples: a light to bring revelation to the Gentiles. And the glory of Your people Israel" (Lk.2:28-32).

The apostle of grace, Peter, who was an agent of His Majesty, elaborated on this topic when he said, "Of this salvation, the prophets have inquired and searched carefully, who prophesied of the grace that would come to you, searching what, or what manner of time the Spirit of Christ who was in them indicating when He testified beforehand the sufferings of Christ and the glories that would follow. To them it was revealed that, not to themselves but to us they were ministering the things which now have been reported to you through those who have preached the gospel to you by the Holy Spirit sent from Heaven – things which even angels desire to look into" (1 Pet.1:10 – 12). In summary, let the Bible speak for itself. "Therefore, if anyone is in Christ, he is a new creation; old things have passed away; behold all things have become new" (2 Cor. 5:17). God is forever doing new things in the lives of His sons and daughters and it is all in and from the mind of God.

Salvation Corner

If you are tired of living the way of sinfulness, remember that God's invitation is still open. Jesus is the gift of God to humanity to join the family of God in heaven and on earth, according to John 3:16. Furthermore, the apostle Paul declared, "I am not ashamed of the gospel of Christ, for it is the power of God to salvation for everyone who believes, for the Jew first and also for the Greek" (Gentile) (Rom.1:16).

The apostle Peter, in support of the above declared: "This is the Stone which was rejected by you builders, which has become the chief cornerstone. Nor is there salvation in any other, for there is no other name under heaven given among men by which we must be saved" (Acts 4:11-12). The verity of Scripture is unequivocally emphatic and sublime.

What do I need to do to be saved?

"The word is near in your mouth and in your heart, (that is the word of faith which we preach): that if you confess with your mouth the Lord Jesus and believe in your heart that God has raised Him from the dead, you will be saved. For with the heart one believes unto righteousness, and with the mouth confession is made unto salvation" (Rom.10:8-10).

Prayer:

Father God, I confess Jesus the Christ as my Lord and Savior. I believe in my heart that He died on the cross of Calvary for my sins. That, on the third day, God raised Him up from the dead for my justification. I now invite you into my heart and ask you to forgive my sins and cleanse me through your blood, and make me your own. I thank You Lord for saving my soul, in Jesus name. Amen.

Repeat the same prayer to receive the baptism of the Holy Spirit. Just as salvation is by faith, so is the promise of the Holy Spirit given to us by faith. The promise is for all who believe in God through Jesus Christ. **So be it.**

What next now that you are born again?

Now, the adventure begins!

References:

Lake, John G. *John G. Lake: His Life, His Sermons, His Boldness of Faith*.

Ft. Worth, TX: Kenneth Copeland Publications, 1994. 196. Print.

Milton Keynes UK
Ingram Content Group UK Ltd.
UKHW010151040424
440506UK00017B/481